Thoughts From the Moon and Sun

Megan chapman

BookLeaf Publishing

India | USA | UK

Presentation by *BookLeaf Publishing*

Web: www.bookleafpub.com

E-mail: info@bookleafpub.com

ISBN: 978-93-5744-947-2

First edition 2022

Passing of Time

Shadows recount the passing of time,
As they crawl misshaped along the wall,
Shades of moonlight blooming hours before
dawn,
The color of dreams turned into shades of love,
The sound of aching silence turned into heart
beats,
A cosmic divide broken like the shades of
shattered moonbeams,
A place made in the shadows just for me.

Taste of Your Name

Romance fades only as time fades
Am I this insane?
Hours have passed, days have come,
But I still remember the taste of your name.

The ghost of your touch—
Left behind a lifetime ago,
Still lingers like a distant echo,
Am I this insane?

To mourn a man I have not met,
A life I have not lived,
I must be insane,
But the taste of your name—
Drives me mad.

The Best of Love

Time passes as night willow blooms,
You make your way across the room,
Glistening in the silver of the moon,
I smell you in the fragrant air,
Like a sin no one else can bare,
A melody only I can hear,
The best of men and best of love,
Isn't this what dreams are made of?
But for every dream there is a price,
And for every wish there is a sacrifice,
When the night willow withers and dies,
So do you return to the moon.

A Dream of Being Whole

I see your face in the shadows of the moon,
Though I have never truly seen you,
I still know the feel of your touch.

memories of love embrace unafraid,
 Alife I have not lived or known,
A dream of holding your hand,
A dream of being whole.

You haunt my dreams,
A shadow unseen,
Holding me while I sleep,
Each night you come alone,
Each morning I wake undone,
Screaming the name of a man I have not known.

The Queen's Slave

The Queen grabbed the moon as the stars
screamed,
Her crimson nails shredding the fabric of the
universe,
She rises twice every day and falls once every
night.

We hear her wails of agony and rejoice in her
battle cry,
We see her silver tear stained face and stamp it
bitter rage,
As if we could know the mind of a Goddess,
As if we should have the right.

We call ourselves Knowledge,
And label our minds Wisdom,
Instead of seeing sadness in her tear stained
eyes--
And the worry on her cheeks.
She carries the madness of the world
And we call it strength,
She carries our insanity and we call it
Boldness.

She grabbed the moon as the stars screamed,

Her crimson nails shredding the fabric of the
universe,
Begging for mercy instead of the vengeance we
crave.

A Tree In the City

The city is too crowded,
Even hours before dawn,
With caffeine mothers, crying children
And fathers stifling yawns,
Staring at screens aand craving dyed eggs,
Complaining about the poor and unfed,
While ignoring the begging man,
Cuz when a tree falls in the city,
-A tree or a man-
The city's swallows the sound of him screaming
As loud as he can

A Hike Before Dawn

Today I went hiking,
Alone and unafraid,
I rose before dusk
And started my day.

I ate apples from a tree,
Growing wild in the city,
Drink water from the fresh springs
Of modern living.

I walk with a deer,
Who told me her name,
I soared with an eagle
Who floated drunken and silly.

I climbed the branches of the
Oldest oak tree,
And stared at the face of our
Galaxy,
And I watched Mother dance
Wild and free.

In 2 or 3 hours,
I experienced a dream
And just before Sun's morning
Rays gleaned,
Made my way back to
Reality.

Tea With the Queen

How rare to see a
theater awaken before dawn,
Trading buckets of dyed popcorn
      - with extra extra butter-
For organic breakfast bagels
      -With extra extra cheese-
Delivered by old fair-haired joe,
A talkative italian fellow
      -from sicily,-
Together we take to the balcony,
Joined by the darkness of a backstreet alley,
      -And rows and rows of seats,=
Just in time for Tea with the Queen.

Plight of the Insomniac

I sit before dawn- a little after 2,
So I've been awake since noon- yesterday,
I leave behind a queen size bed- sheets still
unmade,
And trade them for an old blue chair- who's
fabric is frayed,
Then my eyes are heavy with sleep- a deep and
longing need,
My head and heart ache for adventure- not found
in dreams,
So hours before dawn I travel- instead of sleep,
Learning instead of craving the Zzz's that I need,
Talking to the ancient moon- the ghost banging
on attic walls,
Reading to them the words of Lewis and King -
pondering life and other things,
Writing on them the magic learned from Harry-
fashion learned from Carrie,
The art of painting learned from Caffery and
cooking learned from Jean,
Thinking perhaps I will sleep by noon-
tomorrow.

Icky Cold

On the top of Mount Kilimanjaro,
snow weights down towering pine trees.
Until it collapses under its heave,
And mingles with piles of frozen mud,
That look more like piles of frozen poo,
feeling a natural landfill that never moves,
because -20 is cold. And Icky.

The 5 mile path,
down old Tom's Road,
Leads nowhere in winter,
while the wheat fields are still froze,
and Tom's old tractor is broke,
because walking 10 miles to the store,
In 30 below is icky. And very cold.

nothing blooms in winter,
not even pines that hold the snow,
for even the fish that are left stay below,
because even nature knows winter is
both icky and very, very cold.

Sing to Me Wild Honey Bees

Sing to me, wild honey bees,
By my window under the oak tree,
Land on the roses I planted for thee.

Where have you been
Since this last spring?
What places and lands did you see?
Sing to me wild honey bees

And tell me of your journeys.
From what flowers did you feed?
Land on the roses I planted for thee.

Come and sit with me, please.
I beg of you a moment with me.
Sing to me wild honey bees,

And tell me of the things I long to see,
By my window under the oak tree,
Sing to me wild honey bees.

New Moon Dreams

Hold a browning leaf,
Over the rotting sill.

Let go into the air,
With a wish or prayer.

Call upon your dreams,
And beg they come true.

Watch as the wind catches,
and carries it to a new moon.

Then believe in yourself,
and the power of the new.

Counting 4's

4 hours before 4 a.m.,
Find me staring at shadows
Of the four walls I'm in,
While 4 little girls beg for new retreat,
From 4000 words they're forced to read,
And so I stay 4 hours without sleep.

One glass of cheerwine,
Four apple slices and a bunch of
            pepperoni meat,
Make my entire morning eat,
So I am ready 4 minutes before I am late.

4 little words remind me
To never give up,
With each four words I put to paper,
40 minutes at a time,
Until at last I turn out the four lamped light,
4 hours before 4 a.m. Tonight.

Two Worlds of Mine

In the hot humidity of day,
I am content to be alone,
With nothing but words on blank pages,
And books that feel like home.

In the brittle hours before noon sun,
I am accompanied by Poe and Dickerson,
With tales of love and adventures gone,
Never can I ever be here alone.

But then while between slumbering sheets,
As the moon through clouds and windows peek,
I dream of a world with maybe a little more,
To have someone to share Faulkner and lore.

I spend hours laying awake,
Reaching the likes of Atwood and Hemingway,
To a ghost that does not yet exist,
Pretending I am content with this.

Until the hours creep away,
And dawn draws in another day,

Where I can be content in time,
With the books and words of mine.

17

Ode to the Ghost

I reach across this King size bed,
Wondering what makes California best,
Crossing the chasm of distance between us,
Only to find you've slipped from my fingers,
And I wonder if you were really there at all,
And I wonder If this is what it is like to fall,
In between the cracks of dreams and sanity,
The place where all seems like is reality,
When things only exist in the moonlight,
Just to fade away before morning light.

Ode to the Kitchen

There is but one safe place in all the land,
Where all the problems can be solved,
In between sizzling bacon and buttered eggs,
With a glass of blackened coffee or red merlot,
Or add a spoonful of sugar and a glass of Pinot
Grigio,
Only if you so choose for here it's really up to
you,
Here all the drinks are nectors of the gods,
While we laugh and dream against all odds,
Here nothing in life is ever judged,
Nor is it limited to only a few,
Because in the kitchen love is found,
And peace is summoned over food.

Dancers and Dreams

The drums of salsa float through open doors,
And ushers in the smell of salty shores,
Mingling with the taste of coconut and sweat,
The taste of lust coping as romance,
For the moment, beneath a Pachanga Moon,
Everyone moves to the same rhythm and grove,
Rolling hips to the sound of jazz and blues,
All for the heart of passionate souls,
Looking for a momentary meaning to it all,
This is the life of the dreamer, glorious and bold,
Wrapped in all things beautiful and gold,
Until the Tango sun rises in the morn,
And back to life dreamers must conform.

The Lovers
Unknown Dreams

Never they dream,
Of things worth thinking,
Of books and letters and
Whispers between lovers,
Memories of tender kisses,
Faded lines of poets wishes,
Were his eyes green or blue,
Did he always think of you,
We desire only tender roses,
Of love captured in reality,
Praying that as the morning sun rose,
That we too may have brilliancy,
Beg of we the lovers dreams,
To have all the things we seek,
And lose what makes us feel so weak.

A Hundred and One Lives

Sometimes late at night when I cannot sleep,
I have this strange and wonderful dream,
That I can stand and grasp the sun,
Like a bright light bulb left undone,
I grasp it in the palm of my hand
And turn and turn and turn the sun,
So that the rays spins a hundred times,
And then a hundred times more.
There in the darkness of a moonless night,
I see myself through the sun so bright.

Sometimes the dreams are different,
Like I've lived a hundred lives,
All in the turn of one sleepless night.
Sometimes I'm tired and old and frail,
Watching the shadows of a window veil,
An explorer of the world without a world her
own,
But the best one are the ones Where I smile
 with the dying rage of longest nights,
 In these I find I am the queen of life

October Dreams

I'm dreaming October dreams in the dead of
summer heat,
Crisp autumn nights away from the world,
Bonfires that send shooting stars into the night,
Call of wild mustangs and smell of stale beer,
Midnight howls from bloodhounds that echo in
the hills,
The tinker of bells from cattle grazing in the
field,
When calves are nurse and growing well.
Oh how I long for October dreams.
For I don't like this Summer heat,
No, I don't like it at all.

The Spirits Linger

The spirits linger from room to room,
Never crossing into the next,
Waving to the other spirits
To say hello and good evening,
But they never say more than that.

The spirits linger from room to room,
Each in their own bubble of being,
Distanced from the art of living,
And all but too tired of forgiving.

The spirits linger from room to room,
Forgetting each their own attending,
Forgetting each the others being,
Focused on their own creation.

The spirits linger room to room,
But never say more than that,
All too tired of forgiving,
Focused only on their own creations.